# Polar Animals

Written by Deborah Hodge
Illustrated by Pat Stephens

Kids Can Press

# For Trish, a real Arctic adventurer! – D.H.

# For Caitlin – P.S.

I would like to gratefully acknowledge the thorough review of the manuscript and art by Dr. Laura R. Prugh, Ecologist and Postdoctoral Researcher, Environmental Science, Policy, and Management, at the University of California, Berkeley. Dr. Prugh was formerly with the Biodiversity Centre, Zoology Department, University of British Columbia.

Special thanks to my editor, Stacey Roderick, for her important role in creating this lovely series. Thank you also to editors Lisa Tedesco and Sheila Barry for their ongoing support. To illustrator Pat Stephens and designers Céleste Gagnon and Katie Gray, many thanks for a beautiful book!

---

Text © 2008 Deborah Hodge
Illustrations © 2008 Pat Stephens

Kids Can Press acknowledges the financial support of the Government of Ontario, through the Ontario Media Development Corporation's Ontario Book Initiative; the Ontario Arts Council; the Canada Council for the Arts; and the Government of Canada, through the BPIDP, for our publishing activity.

Published in Canada by
Kids Can Press Ltd
29 Birch Avenue
Toronto, ON  M4V 1E2

Published in the U.S. by
Kids Can Press Ltd.
2250 Military Road
Tonawanda, NY  14150

www.kidscanpress.com

Kids Can Press is a *corus*™ Entertainment company

Edited by Stacey Roderick
Designed by Céleste Gagnon and Katie Gray
Printed and bound in Singapore

The hardcover edition of this book is smyth sewn casebound. The paperback edition of this book is limp sewn with a drawn-on cover.

CM 08  0 9 8 7 6 5 4 3 2 1
CM PA 08  0 9 8 7 6 5 4 3 2 1

**Library and Archives Canada Cataloguing in Publication**
Hodge, Deborah
Polar animals / written by Deborah Hodge ;
illustrated by Pat Stephens.

(Who lives here?)
ISBN 978-1-55453-043-4 (bound)
ISBN 978-1-55453-044-1 (pbk.)

1. Animals—Polar regions—Juvenile literature. I. Stephens, Pat, 1950–
II. Title. III. Series: Hodge, Deborah.  Who lives here?

QL112.H63 200        j591.75'86        C2007-902960-4

# Contents

# What Is a Polar Region?

A polar region is a very cold place. For most of the year, thick snow and ice cover the ground. Oceans freeze and fierce winds blow. The Arctic and Antarctic are polar regions.

The Arctic is home to many amazing creatures. Like all polar animals, their bodies are built for living in the cold.

Brr! Antarctica is the coldest place on Earth. Whales, seals and seabirds are the only large animals that can live here.

Some polar animals live on pack ice — large areas of sea ice floating in the ocean.

Arctic land is called tundra. Caribou and other animals gobble up plants that grow here in the short summer.

# Emperor Penguin

The emperor penguin lives in chilly Antarctica. These penguins are taller than a kitchen table.

A mother and father emperor penguin take turns looking after their baby. The chick sits on its parents' feet, up off the icy ground.

Waterproof feathers overlap tightly and cover the penguin like a thick winter coat.

Emperor penguins huddle for warmth. They take turns in the middle where it is warmest.

A penguin uses its wings to swim. It speeds through the ocean hunting for fish. Zoom!

# Arctic Fox

The arctic fox is the size of a small dog. It roams over snow and ice hunting for lemmings and other prey.

An arctic fox's fur is the warmest of any animal. The white color blends in with the snow and helps the fox hide from snowy owls and other enemies.

The fox uses its tail to cover its face like a cozy scarf while it sleeps. Zzz ...

Thick fur grows on the top and bottom of the fox's paws to keep its feet warm.

Like all arctic foxes, this young pup's fur will change to white when winter comes.

# Seal

The seal is an excellent swimmer. Seals have smooth bodies that glide easily through the polar oceans.

Some seals live under the ice for most of the year. In spring, a mother gives birth on the ice but quickly returns to the sea with her pup.

Swinging its back flippers from side to side, a seal races through the ocean hunting for fish.

A seal uses its sharp claws or teeth to cut a breathing hole in the ice. Now it can pop up and breathe.

Some pups are born inside a snow den. Shh ... It's a good place to hide from hungry polar bears.

# Snowy Owl

The snowy owl is a fierce hunter. These owls perch on rocks and hills on the tundra to watch for their prey.

Whoosh! With its big wings outstretched, a snowy owl swoops down on lemmings, birds, hares and other small animals.

Snowy owls use sharp claws called talons to catch lemmings and other prey.

The owl's white feathers blend in with the snowy land and help it stay hidden.

Dark feathers match the colors of the tundra and help young owlets hide from enemies.

# Musk Ox

The musk ox has long, shaggy fur to keep it warm. Musk oxen live on the tundra in big groups called herds.

Mmm ... A baby musk ox stays close to its mother to keep snug and warm until its own long fur grows in.

Soft, short fur under the long fur gives extra protection against the wind and cold.

Male musk oxen butt heads and horns to decide who is the biggest and strongest.

A musk ox uses its big front hoof like a shovel to dig up tasty plants buried under the snow.

15

# Beluga Whale

The beluga whale swims in the icy Arctic Ocean. Belugas eat fish and other creatures that live in the water.

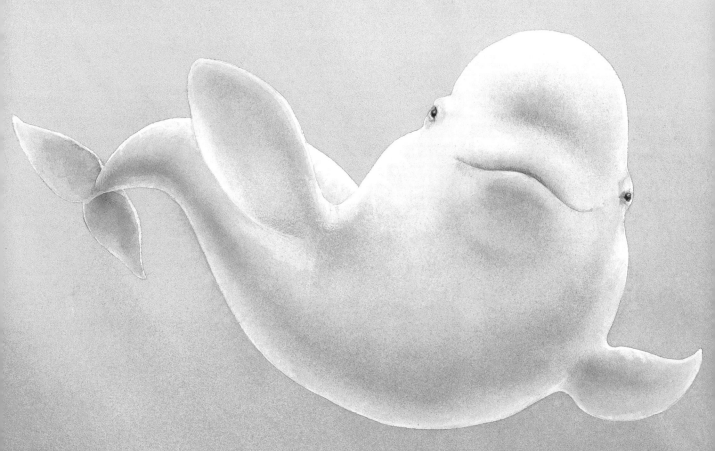

A beluga lives in a group called a pod. The whales in the pod talk to each other using sounds such as chirps, whistles and squeals.

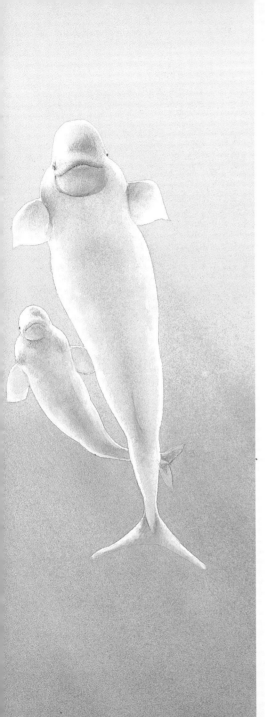

A beluga breathes through a hole on the top of its head. Belugas poke their heads out of the water to get air.

Blubber, a thick layer of fat under the beluga's skin, works like a warm blanket to keep out the cold. Ahh ...

As a baby beluga gets older, its gray skin will turn white like its parents.

# Polar Bear

The polar bear is a powerful hunter. Polar bears prowl over pack ice and swim in the ocean hunting for seals.

Polar bear cubs are born in a snow den. When they are old enough, their mother teaches them how to hunt and stay safe.

A hungry polar bear waits by a breathing hole. When a seal comes up for air, the bear pounces!

A layer of blubber under the polar bear's skin keeps it warm in ice cold water. Splish, splash!

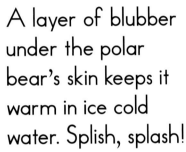

Polar bears can run very fast. Fur on the bottom of each paw keeps them from slipping.

# Walrus

The walrus is a large animal with long teeth called tusks. Walruses live in the freezing polar water near pack ice.

Walruses spend most of their time in the chilly ocean but climb onto ice or rocky shores to rest and give birth.

A baby walrus doesn't have much blubber. The calf stays warm snuggled next to its mother.

The walrus jabs its strong tusks into the ice to help pull its heavy body out of the water.

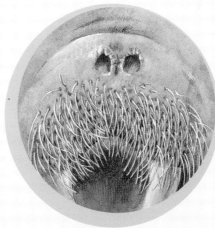

A walrus uses its whiskers like fingers to feel along the dark ocean bottom for clams and other food. Gulp!

# Caribou

The caribou is a fast runner. Each spring, huge herds of caribou cross tundra and rivers to find new plants to eat.

A mother caribou gives birth to her baby on the long journey. The calf is ready to run just a few hours after being born.

A caribou is a strong swimmer. It uses its feet as paddles to pull itself through the water.

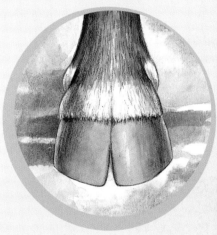

Caribou hooves work like snowshoes. They spread wide to keep the caribou on top of the snow.

Long legs help the caribou run fast and escape from hungry wolves. Hurry!

# Animal Words

Every polar animal has special body parts that help it get food and stay warm and safe. Can you find pictures of these body parts in the book?

 **blubber** page 17

 **feathers** page 7

 **flippers** page 11

 **fur** page 15

 **hoof** page 23

 **talons** page 13

## For Parents and Teachers

The Arctic, at the North Pole, is a huge, frozen ocean surrounded by land called tundra, while Antarctica, at the South Pole, is an ice-covered continent circled by oceans. Polar animals are well adapted to the extreme cold, dryness and wind in these places. Penguins are found only in the Antarctic, while seals and whales live in both the Arctic and Antarctic. The beluga whale and the rest of the animals in this book are from the Arctic. (Fewer species live in the Antarctic due to the extreme cold that occurs there.)

Scientists are concerned that pollution and global warming are affecting the world's polar regions. Shrinking polar ice, resulting from warmer temperatures, contributes to an unstable food supply for polar animals. As a result, some species such as the polar bear are becoming endangered.